CATS

ABYSSINIAN CATS

STUART A. KALLEN
ABDO & Daughters

Published by Abdo & Daughters, 4940 Viking Drive, Suite 622, Edina, Minnesota 55435.

Library bound edition distributed by Rockbottom Books, Pentagon Tower, P.O. Box 36036, Minneapolis, Minnesota 55435.

Printed in the United States.

Cover Photo credit: Peter Arnold, Inc.
Interior Photo credits: Peter Arnold, Inc. pages 5, 11, 21

Animals, Animals, pages 7, 9, 13, 15, 19

Edited by Rosemary Wallner

Library of Congress Cataloging-in-Publication Data

Kallen, Stuart A., 1955
    Abyssinian cat / Stuart A. Kallen.
    p. cm. — (Cats)
    Includes bibliographical references (p.24) and index.
    ISBN 1-56239-446-0
1. Abyssinian cat—Juvenile literature. [1. Abyssinian cat. 2. Cats.] I. Title. II.
Series: Kallen, Stuart A., 1955- Cats.
SF449.A28K35   1995
636.8'26—dc20
                                        95-10526
                                           CIP
                                           AC

ABOUT THE AUTHOR

Stuart Kallen has written over 80 children's books, including many environmental science books.

Contents

LIONS, TIGERS, AND CATS

Few animals are as beautiful and graceful as cats. And all cats are related. From the wild lions of Africa to the common house cat, all belong to the family **Felidae**. Cats are found almost everywhere. They include cheetahs, jaguars, lynx, ocelots, and **domestic** cats.

People first domesticated cats around 5,000 years ago in the Middle East. Although humans have tamed them, house cats still think and act like their bigger cousins.

All cats are related, from the wild cheetahs of Africa to the common house cat.

ABYSSINIAN CATS

Through the centuries, Abyssinians (ab-uh-SIN-ee-ans), which look like African wild cats, have charmed many people. The **ancient** Egyptians worshipped cats that looked like the Abyssinian. The **breed** is believed to be one of the oldest **domestic** cats.

The cat's name comes from Abyssinia, the former name of Ethiopia, a country in Africa. People first brought cats from Abyssinia to Great Britain in 1868.

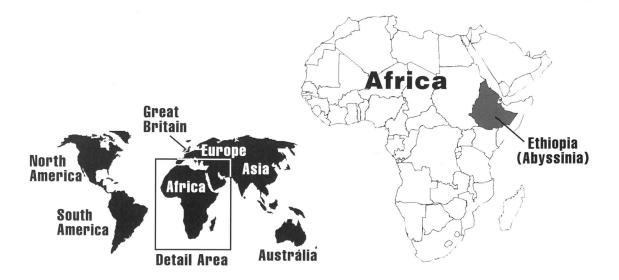

The Abyssinian gets its name from Abyssinia,
the former name of Ethiopia.

WHAT THEY'RE LIKE

Abyssinian cats, or "Abys," are alert and smart. They have a sweet **temperament** and will come if called. They are lively and athletic. But they do not like living in small apartments. Abys also have one trait you don't often see in cats. They like to swim in water.

Abyssinian cats are alert, smart and have sweet temperaments.

COAT AND COLOR

Abys are known as "rabbit cats" because their fur looks like rabbit fur. An Aby's **coat** is glossy and soft. Two or three bands of color appear over a darker base.

Today, there are several types of Aby coloring: ruddy (ruddy brown and black), red (copper and chocolate), blue (warm blue gray), lilac (light pinkish gray), silver (silver and black), and silver sorrel (silvery peach and chocolate).

Abyssinian cats are known as "rabbit cats" because their fur looks like rabbit fur.

SIZE

Abys are graceful and well-muscled. They are medium in length with small oval-shaped feet. They have long, fine-boned legs. The cats look like they are standing on tiptoe. Abys have a round head. Their large almond-shaped eyes can be green, amber, or hazel.

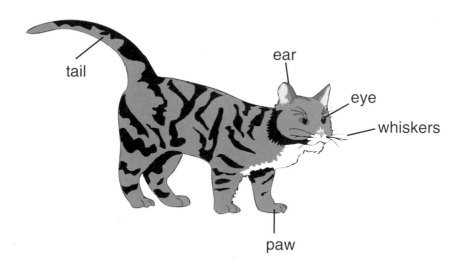

Most cats share the same features.

Abyssinian cats have large almond-shaped eyes that can be green, amber, or hazel.

CARE

Like all cats, Abys love a good brushing. Besides making the cat purr, brushing the cat will keep its loose hair off the furniture. **Grooming** an Aby will also keep **hair balls** from forming.

Like any pet, Abys need love and attention. Cats make fine pets. But they still have some of their wild **instincts**.

Cats are natural hunters and do well exploring outdoors. A scratching post where the cat can sharpen its claws saves furniture from damage.

Cats bury their waste and should be trained to use a litter box. Clean the box every day. Cats love to play. A ball, **catnip**, or a loose string will keep a kitten busy for hours.

Like any pet, Abyssinian cats need love and attention. Cats make fine pets, but they still have some of their wild instincts.

FEEDING

Cats eat fish and meat. Hard bones that do not splinter help keep the cat's teeth and mouth clean. Water should always be available. Most cats thrive on dried cat food. Kittens drink their mother's milk. However, milk can cause illness in adult cats.

Like all cats, Abyssinians love milk. But
sometimes milk can cause illness.

KITTENS

Female cats are **pregnant** for about 65 days. They can have two to eight kittens. The average cat has four kittens.

Kittens are blind and helpless for the first several weeks. After about three weeks they will start crawling and playing. At this time they may be given cat food.

After about a month, kittens will run, wrestle, and play games. If the cat is a **pedigree**, it should be registered and given papers at this time. At 10 weeks the kittens are old enough to be sold or given away.

A female Abyssinian cat cleaning her kittens.

BUYING A KITTEN

The best place to buy an Abyssinian cat is from a **breeder**. Cat shows are also good places to find kittens.

Next, you must decide if you want a simple pet or a show winner. A basic Aby can cost $150, with blue-ribbon winners costing as much as $1,000. When you buy an Abyssinian, you should also file **pedigree** papers that register the animal with the Cat Fanciers Association.

When buying a kitten, check it closely for signs of good health. The ears, nose, mouth, and fur should be clean. Eyes should be bright and clear. The cat should be alert and interested in its surroundings. A healthy kitten will move around with its head held high.

Abyssinian cat and kitten.

GLOSSARY

ANCIENT - Very old.

BREED - To raise or grow; also, a kind or type.

BREEDER - A person who breeds animals or plants.

CATNIP - A strong-smelling plant used as stuffing for cat toys.

COAT - An animal's outer covering (fur).

DOMESTICATE (doe-MESS-tih-kate) - To tame or adapt to home life.

FELIDAE (FEE-lih-day) - The Latin name given to the cat family.

GROOMING - Cleaning.

HAIR BALLS - Balls of fur that gather in a cat's stomach after grooming itself by licking.

INSTINCT - A way of acting that is born in an animal, not learned.

PEDIGREE - A record of an animal's ancestors.

PREGNANT - With one or more babies growing inside the body.

TEMPERAMENT - An animal's nature.

Index

BIBLIOGRAPHY

Alderton, David. *Cats*. New York: Dorling Kindersley, 1992.

Clutton-Brock, Juliet. *Cat*. New York: Alfred A. Knopf, 1991.

DePrisco, Andrew. *The Mini-Atlas of Cats*. Neptune City, N.J.: T.F.H. Publications, 1991.

Taylor, David. *The Ultimate Cat Book*. New York: Simon & Schuster, 1989.